REVIEW C

W9-CFB-553

NOT CHOSEN FOR REVIEW

TPS Surplus
NSFSLU

TPS Surplus
NSFSLU

STADIUM

Collective Biographies

TPS Surplus
NSFSLU

American Dinosaur Hunters

Nathan Aaseng

Enslow Publishers, Inc.

44 Fadem Road	PO Box 38
Box 699	Aldershot
Springfield, NJ 07081	Hants GU12 6BP
USA	UK

FEB / / 2000

Copyright © 1996 by Nathan Aaseng

All rights reserved.

No part of this book may be reproduced by any means
without the written permission of the publisher.

Library of Congress Cataloging-in-Publication Data

Aaseng, Nathan.
    American dinosaur hunters / Nathan Aaseng.
       p. cm. —(Collective biographies)
    Includes bibliographical references and index.
    Summary: Profiles the lives of ten important paleontologists, including
Edward Hitchcock, Joseph Leidy, Barnum Brown, Roy Chapman Andrews,
and Jack Horner.
    ISBN 0-89490-710-7
    1. Paleontologists—United States—Biography—Juvenile literature.
[1. Paleontologists.] 1. Title. II. Series.
QE707.A2A27 1996
560'.92'2—dc20
[B]   96-6056
                                CIP
                                AC

Printed in the United States of America

10 9 8 7 6 5 4 3 2 1

Illustration Credits: Academy of Natural Sciences, Philadelphia, pp. 16, 22,
24; American Museum of Natural History, pp. 48, 52, 76, 80; American
Heritage Center, p. 45; Canadian Museum of Nature, pp. 58, 63;
Dinamation International Society (1-800-DIG-DINO), p. 86; Library of
Congress, pp. 8, 12, 26, 38; Museum of the Rockies, pp. 94, 100; National
Park Service, pp. 66, 70, 74; Courtesy of Peabody Museum, Yale
University, 33.

Cover Illustrations: Dinamation International Society (1-800-DIG-DINO)
(inset); George White Photography (background).

Contents

Introduction

We know that huge beasts called dinosaurs dominated the earth for 170 million years. Even young children today have a good idea what dinosaurs looked like, where they lived, what they ate, and even how some of them cared for their young.

The discovery of dinosaur facts ranks among the greatest detective work of all time, because the dinosaur trail is about as cold as a trail can get. The last dinosaur disappeared approximately 65 million years ago. The only pieces of evidence that dinosaurs ever existed are fossils—mostly bones, teeth, eggs, and foot imprints buried in the rock.

Before the nineteenth century, no one knew that dinosaurs once roamed the earth. People had known about fossils since the Stone Age, but throughout the centuries, those who discovered strange bones and markings in stone had no clear idea of what these things were. Archaeologists have discovered that early humans worked dinosaur eggshells into mosaic squares.

Spanish explorers in the sixteenth century were baffled when Native Americans showed them huge fossil bones. The Plains Indians believed that these monstrous bones were the remains of the grandfather of the buffalo.

Europeans, however, could not easily accept this idea. They thought God would not allow his creations to become extinct. If these were indeed bones of living things, then the offspring of these giant beasts must still be around, they thought. Despite worldwide exploration, though, these giants were nowhere to be found. Some Europeans proposed that the fossils were merely divine ornaments—meant to decorate the earth below the ground as flowers decorate the earth's surface.

As more types of huge fossil bones turned up, however, European scientists began to accept the idea that fossils were the remains of life forms that had died out. The study of fossils, called paleontology, became a popular field of study in Western Europe in the late eighteenth century.

At that time, Americans were spectators in the detective work going on with fossils. Most fossils found in America were sent to Europe for the experts to examine.

Thomas Jefferson, who collected fossils as a hobby, helped spark American interest in fossils. In 1797, Jefferson wrote a paper entitled "A Memoir on the Discovery of Certain Bones of a Quadruped of the Clawed Kind in the Western Parts of Virginia."[1] He helped make paleontology respectable in the United States by keeping a fossil collection in the White House after he was elected president in 1801. When he sent Lewis and Clark on their expedition to explore the West, Jefferson hoped they might find live specimens of the great "elephant" whose fossils he owned.

In the 1820s, European experts examined some bones found in England and concluded that they were the remains of two types of large, lizardlike animals. They named these animals *Megalosaurus* (giant lizard) and *Iguanodon* (iguana tooth). Scientists use Latin names to classify organisms. In 1841, English scientist Richard Owen proposed the name *dinosaur*, meaning "terrible reptiles," to describe these animals.

Dinosaurs appeared to have been rare creatures, confined to Europe. No one had described any such lizardlike bones in North America, and there was no reason to suspect they ever would.

In fact, William Clark had collected fossils of unusual marine reptiles on his explorations. (He mistakenly thought they were fishbones.) Beginning in the 1830s, Americans began to gather clues that would later show that a fascinating mix of prehistoric creatures had once lived in North America as well as in Europe.

This book tells the story of some of those American dinosaur hunters. Some of them braved heat, thirst, hunger, rugged mountains, and hostile neighbors to scour bleak, remote lands in search of dinosaur remains hidden in the rocks. Others studied the fossils unearthed by others and made sense of the often confusing assortments of bone, teeth, and imprints. Over the next 160 years, these

American dinosaur hunters and detectives would be largely responsible for piecing together those clues to provide a vivid picture of the breathtaking variety of giant animals that once walked the planet.

The hunt for dinosaurs is far from over. Dinosaur hunters continue to uncover more clues about the nature of dinosaurs. As the work of Robert Bakker and Jack Horner proves, even today there is no limit to what a keen eye and a bright mind can discover about the creatures who ruled our planet for millions of years.

Edward Hitchcock

Edward Hitchcock
On the Wrong Track

The first solid evidence of dinosaurs in North America came not from bones but from footprints. Edward Hitchcock knew more about fossil footprints than any other person alive in the mid-nineteenth century. However, even the experts make mistakes. Hitchcock died without ever knowing that he had uncovered evidence that dinosaurs once lived in North America.

Edward Hitchcock was born in Deerfield, Massachusetts, in 1793. His father was a hatter, which may have accounted for Edward's poor health during childhood. Arsenic, a poisonous substance, was commonly used in the preparation of hats and may have affected Edward.[1]

Young Edward was fascinated by science. While

still a teenager, he published an article about his observations on comets. A local publisher found out to his sorrow how capable and thorough young Hitchcock could be. The publisher offer a reward to anyone who could find any errors in the math tables of his new nautical almanac. He withdrew the offer when Hitchcock detected eighty mistakes!

At this time, the only professions that offered scientific training were the fields of medicine and religion. After serving as principal of Deerfield Academy, Hitchcock went on to study theology in New Haven, Connecticut. There he came in contact with some of the best scientific minds in the country.

After serving as a Congregational minister, Hitchcock signed on in 1825 as a professor of chemistry and natural history at Amherst College in Amherst, Massachusetts. He stayed there for the remainder of his career, serving for many years as the college president.

In 1835, Hitchcock became curious about the strange fossil tracks in the Connecticut Valley. He must have heard about these tracks for many years. He was ten years old when college student Pliny Moody plowed up the first of these while tilling his father's field near South Hadley, Massachusetts. Moody had turned up a slab of sandstone on which he found the clear imprint of a large three-toed foot. The tracks were like those of a bird, only larger. Over the years, several other tracks were discovered in the area. Some tracks measured more than a foot and a half (a half meter) across.

People attempted to explain these enormous tracks. Some guessed that the tracks were made by a giant turkey. Others claimed the huge tracks were made by the great raven that Noah had sent to find land when the world was flooded, according to the Bible story.

Hitchcock was not content with speculating about the nature of the tracks. Each summer he scoured the Connecticut Valley, looking for fossilized bird tracks. As his interest in tracks became known, others alerted him to new sources of tracks. Hitchcock found some in unexpected places. For example, one specimen came from a street where it had been used as pavement for sixty years.

Over the years, Hitchcock collected roughly eight thousand fossil tracks. A wealthy Boston man donated funds to house the collection in a special cabinet on the Amherst campus.

As Hitchcock studied his fossils, he saw that they were made by at least seven different creatures. He divided the tracks into two major groups: those with thick toes and those with thin ones. In 1841, he published a book describing in detail the nature of these strange fossil tracks.

Hitchcock was not content merely to record the scientific evidence. What excited him about fossil tracks was imagining what the owners of the tracks looked like. He enjoyed, as he wrote, "the privilege

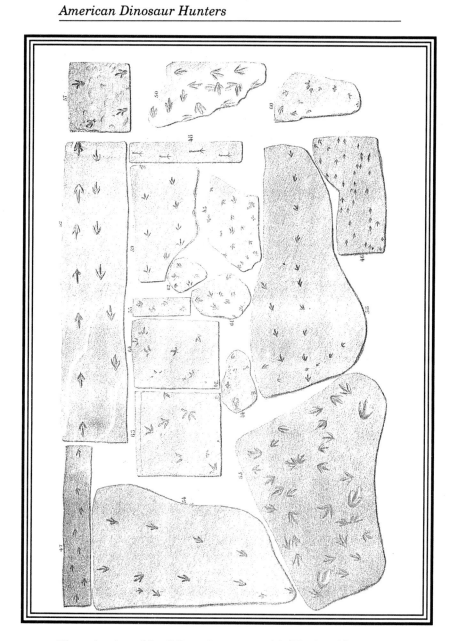

These sketches of fossil footprints appeared in Hitchcock's report on the geology of Massachusetts, published in 1841.

of gazing upon them, and of bringing into view one lost form after another."[2]

Footprints were only a small clue from which to piece together a picture of these lost forms. They showed that these creatures were huge and unlike any living animal—but what were they?

As early as 1837, Hitchcock wondered if the creatures who made his tracks were related to the strange gigantic lizards found in Europe. In describing one track, he said that it "certainly looks more like the forefoot of a lizard . . . than the arm of a bird."[3]

Most of the tracks looked like bird tracks. Most important, they were made by an animal that walked on two legs, as a bird does. In contrast, the only two dinosaurs discovered at that time appeared to have walked on four legs as lizards do. Furthermore, Hitchcock knew that very large birds such as ostriches existed. A British surgeon had also discovered giant eggs and the bones of what was clearly a bird that must have stood 12 feet (4 meters) high.

Unfortunately for Hitchcock, no fossil bones had turned up in the Connecticut Valley that might be connected to the tracks. He had no reason to suspect that the *Megalosaurus* and *Iguanodon* fossils found in Europe had any relatives in North America.

In the absence of supporting evidence, Hitchcock concluded that most of the tracks were left by birds. He wrote, "Now I have seen, in scientific vision, an apterous [wingless] bird, some twelve, fifteen feet high—nay large flocks of them—walking over the muddy surface."[4] He gave these birds names such as *Ornithictnites gigantieus* (giant bird).

Hitchcock accomplished much beyond the study of fossil tracks. He took charge of the first state geological survey of Massachusetts and Vermont, wrote a geology textbook, and helped to found the American Association for the Advancement of Science. Giant bird tracks were his lifelong passion, however. He spent the last thirty years of his life collecting, describing, and analyzing the tracks. Even when he struggled with poor health in his final years, Hitchcock kept at the task.

In 1861, rock hunters uncovered clues that might have put the old fossil track expert on the right track at last. German researchers discovered a well-preserved skeleton of an *Archaeopteryx* (ancient feather), a feathered creature with the body of a reptile. As the *Archaeopteryx* appeared to have lived millions of years ago, it provided some evidence that birdlike reptiles could have made the footprints that Hitchcock found. British scientist Thomas Huxley pointed out the many similarities between birds and reptiles and suggested that they might be related. By this time, dinosaur bones had been found in North America as well as Europe.

Hitchcock never saw the connection between the large, extinct dinosaurs and his bird tracks. He saw *Archaeopteryx* as evidence that many fascinating birds lived in the ancient world when the footprints were made. At the end of his life, he wrote a long book in which he discussed all that he had learned in his study of tracks. In 1864, just a few months after completing the book, Edward Hitchcock died, without realizing that he had been the first American to study and describe the remains of dinosaurs in North America.

Joseph Leidy

Joseph Leidy
The Pit at Haddonfield

Joseph Leidy just did not have what it took to be successful as a medical doctor. He knew as well as anyone how the human body was put together, but he could not make a living putting his medical training to use. Instead, he turned his attention to the bones of creatures that had been dead and turned to stone millions of years ago. In so doing, Leidy alerted the world to the fact that dinosaurs were not rare freaks of nature. He discovered that these incredible beasts once had thrived in many parts of the world.

Joseph Leidy was born in Philadelphia, in 1823. By strange coincidence, he was the son of a hatter, as was Hitchcock. Leidy's mother died before Joseph reached his second birthday. She was exceptional for a woman of her time in that she was far more educated than her German immigrant husband.

Joseph's father wanted his children to be educated, as his wife had been. He worked hard so that Joseph could enroll in private schools. Joseph, however, did not share his father's enthusiasm for education. He preferred exploring the natural outdoor world to studying the school's primary subjects: Greek and Latin. Frequently, he skipped class.

When Leidy chose to apply himself, he was a brilliant student. He attended the University of Pennsylvania in Philadelphia, and earned a degree in medicine at the age of twenty-one. Because the young doctor was not able to build a successful practice, he gave up dealing with patients in 1848 and went back to school, this time as an instructor at Franklin Medical College. He demonstrated such a keen understanding of anatomy, the study of how organisms are put together, that the University of Pennsylvania hired him as a professor. While at the school, Leidy wrote a valuable medical textbook on human anatomy. A modest, gentle, dignified man, he was well liked by his colleagues and students.

Leidy was interested not only in the structure of humans but in the structure of anything in nature, living or nonliving. He studied plants, animals, microscopic creatures called protozoa, and even minerals. This passion for scientific knowledge led him to become an active member of the Academy of Natural Sciences in Philadelphia.

He joined with others of the academy to purchase a fossil of a jawbone and some sharp teeth that had been found on Prince Edward Island in Canada. Leidy used his knowledge of anatomy to compare the fossil to the bones and teeth of other animals. He noticed similarities between the fossil and Europe's *Megalosaurus,* as well as present-day lizards. Leidy wondered if there might be some connection between this beast and Hitchcock's giant tracks, but he did not have enough evidence to draw any conclusions. He simply called the fossil creature *Bathygnathus borealis* (northern deep jaw).

The experience raised Leidy's curiosity about fossils. He became friends with Spencer Baird of the new Smithsonian Institute. Baird arranged for Leidy to take part in a fossil-collecting expedition to the West in 1852. On the night before Leidy was to start out on the trip, however, he received tragic news. Dr. Horner, the university's professor of anatomy, had become fatally ill. Leidy had to stay behind and take over Horner's classes. Leidy never got another opportunity to take part in a major expedition into the fossil fields of the West. He had to content himself with analyzing the bones that others brought to him.

In 1854, Leidy moved on to Swarthmore College to serve as professor of natural history. A couple of years later, he was asked to take a look at some fossil teeth that had been found in the wilderness of what is now Montana. The teeth were collected in 1855 by Dr. Ferdinand Hayden during a U.S. Army exploring and mapping expedition.

Leidy found a strong resemblance between these teeth and European fossil teeth. Despite the lack of supporting evidence, he felt confident enough in the similarities to declare that Hayden had found the teeth of a plant-eating dinosaur. Leidy named the dinosaur *Trachodon* (rough tooth). Leidy's description of the dinosaur was groundbreaking news among scientists. If Leidy was correct, then dinosaurs lived not only in a small section of Northern Europe but also across the ocean in North America. They could well have been successful animals who roamed across the entire earth.

Leidy had gone out on a limb by basing this declaration of dinosaurs in North America on so little evidence. In order to win over skeptics, he had to come up with more complete fossil evidence. That soon appeared, thanks to William Foulke, a member of the Academy of Natural Sciences. Foulke spent his summers and autumns across the Delaware River from Philadelphia, near the town of Haddonfield, New Jersey. He heard from his New Jersey neighbors about some huge bones that had been dug out of a quarry on the farm of John Hopkins twenty years earlier. Foulke decided to investigate.

The bones were long gone, however. Visitors and workmen had carried them off, and Hopkins could not begin to guess where they might be. Foulke could not even find the old pit from which the bones had come. Over the course of twenty years, the pit had eroded and become overgrown with plants.

At last Foulke found one of the men who had been hired to do the digging twenty years earlier. He was able to locate the pit in a narrow ravine. Foulke got Hopkins's permission to dig on the land and hired a crew to do the job. After a great deal of digging, the crew struck a pile of large bones.

Foulke sent the bones to Leidy. Leidy sorted out nine teeth, twenty-eight vertebrae from the backbone, fragments of a lower jaw, and assorted bones from the limbs and pelvis. There was enough for him to make a good guess as to how the creature's skeleton was put together.

Leidy found that the animal was 26 to 30 feet (8 to 9 meters) long. Furthermore, the structure of the bones was similar to those of the European dinosaur, *Iguanodon.* This time, Leidy was on solid ground in claiming that dinosaurs had lived in North America. He had a dinosaur skeleton from New Jersey even more complete than the dinosaur skeletons from Europe. Leidy named the creature *Hadrosaurus,* after the town of Haddonfield, where it was found.

Leidy's study of *Hadrosaurus* uncovered a startling fact. The creature's front limbs were shorter than its back limbs. In fact, the difference was so great, said Leidy, that if the bones had not been found together, he would have thought they were from different animals. Leidy concluded that

The skeleton of *Hadrosaurus* was displayed at the Academy of Natural Sciences in Philadelphia.

Hadrosaurus did not lumber along on four legs, as all dinosaurs were thought to do. Rather it must have spent at least some time on its hind legs. Leidy proposed that it might have eaten tree leaves "in the habit of browsing, sustaining itself kangaroo-like in erect position," that is, standing on its back legs and tail.[1]

Leidy also took an educated guess about where *Hadrosaurus* preferred to live. It was obviously a land creature, yet the *Hadrosaurus* was found in rocks made from ancient ocean deposits. Since *Hadrosaurus* bones rarely showed up in such deposits, Leidy concluded that "those in our possession had been carried down the current of a river, upon whose banks the animals lived."[2]

Leidy's brilliant analysis of the *Hadrosaurus* bones earned him fame as the United States expert on fossil bones. He was the person to whom fossil collectors throughout the nation sent their finds for identification. As he did not marry until the age of forty and had no children, Leidy had plenty of time to pursue this fascinating subject.

He might have gone on to reveal a great many things about the mysterious extinct giants, but he was undercut while at the peak of his abilities. In the 1870s, O. C. Marsh and Edward Cope began paying large sums of money for fossils. Leidy did not have the funds to compete with them. Few fossil hunters would send a find to Leidy when they could collect money by sending it to Marsh or Cope.

In the wake of the coming "Bone Wars," the discovery of America's first dinosaur was soon forgotten.

Leidy was pushed into the background during the great dinosaur discoveries of the 1870s. He was so appalled by the outrageous behavior of Cope and Marsh in their competition for dinosaur bones that he wanted nothing more to do with the entire profession. Joseph Leidy, the man who first alerted the world to the worldwide reign of dinosaurs, gave up the study of fossil bones altogether. He spent his time probing a variety of scientific subjects, and he died in 1891.

Othniel Charles Marsh

O. C. Marsh
The Bone Wars, Part I

Prior to the 1870s, many people doubted that dinosaurs had once existed. They did not trust the few scattered bits of evidence produced by scientists. The 1870s produced such an avalanche of evidence about dinosaurs, though, that most people came to accept them.

How this avalanche of information came about is one of the more embarrassing episodes in American scientific history. A bitter feud between O. C. Marsh and Edward Cope drove each man to a furious effort to unlock the secrets of the past. These two wealthy men engaged in a no-holds-barred, mudslinging, back-stabbing race to see who could get the biggest, best, and most unusual fossils. Their private bone war unearthed fossil bones by the ton. Every new creature they found seemed to be more spectacular and unusual than the last.

Othniel Charles Marsh was born in Lockport, New York, in 1831. In another coincidence he, like Leidy, lost his mother at any early age. Marsh spent a lonely childhood with his father, a struggling farmer, and various uncles, aunts, and a stepmother.

Marsh was not a sharp student. He showed little ambition throughout his youth, but he took full advantage of his wealthy uncle, George. George Peabody, a bachelor who made his fortune in banking and business, liked to promote education. In 1852, he sent his twenty-year-old nephew money earmarked for the boy's education. This enabled Marsh to enroll at the Phillips Academy in Massachusetts.

Marsh had much ground to make up in his studies. While most of his classmates graduated as teenagers, Marsh did not finish at Phillips until he was twenty-five. Backed by Peabody's money, he then enrolled in Yale University. Marsh was so much older than his fellow Yale students that they nicknamed him Daddy. He plodded through his studies, taking six years to complete his degree.

By that time the Civil War was raging. Marsh sailed to Europe to continue his studies. Some historians claim he did so to avoid fighting; others say his poor eyesight disqualified him from fighting.

At any rate, he visited his uncle George in London and made plans to continue in a field of study that had long fascinated him. As a teenager, Marsh had collected fossils dug up by workers who were digging the Erie Canal near the Marsh home. Now that Leidy had shown that dinosaurs had lived in North America, Marsh was convinced that there were a great number of fossils waiting to be discovered. He talked his uncle into contributing $150,000 to Yale for the purpose of starting a museum that would include fossils.

Yale rewarded Marsh with a post by putting him in charge of the museum as a professor with no teaching duties. He lived the life of a gentleman in a luxurious eighteen-room house in New Haven, Connecticut. Marsh never married. With plenty of time on his hands and his uncle's money to spend, he was in an ideal situation to pursue his love of fossils.

Marsh became friends with a brilliant young fossil expert, Edward Cope. In 1867, Cope paid Marsh the compliment of naming a new fossil species after Marsh, and Marsh later returned the favor. In 1868, the two spent a week together poking around the digs at Haddonfield.

The promising friendship quickly crumbled. Marsh's personality contributed to what became an intense feud. Marsh was a self-centered man, used to getting his way through his uncle's money and prestige. He did not work well with people and had no close friends throughout his life.

When it came to fossils, Marsh was terribly possessive and suspected virtually everyone of trying to get what he had. According to one colleague, Marsh "entered every field of acquisition with the dominating ambition to obtain everything there was in it and leave not a single scrap behind."[1] He was paranoid about other scientists. When he allowed them to visit his museum, he would put on his slippers and sneak after them to make sure they went only in rooms where they were allowed.

When Marsh's personality rubbed against Cope's equally prickly nature, fireworks erupted. Their letters to each other began to include insulting comments about each other's mistakes. Marsh ridiculed an error that Cope had made in putting the head where the tail should have gone when he restored a skeleton of a marine reptile. Before long, Marsh and Cope were enemies.

In 1868, Marsh took his first trip into the fossil fields of the western United States. In western Nebraska, a railroad stationmaster presented him with a fossil that Marsh later identified as a tiny ancient horse. Scientists regarded this horse as solid evidence of evolution. Marsh became famous as a result of this find, and he returned to the West four times with Yale students in pursuit of fossils.

The bone war between Cope and Marsh heated up in 1872, when both men were exploring Wyoming. Cope hired one of Marsh's men to show him Marsh's digging sites. A few weeks later, Cope published an article on extinct mammals. Marsh, who guarded his digging sites jealously, accused Cope of invading his turf to get the information for that article. He complained that Cope had stolen "more than half the discoveries for which I have risked my life."[2]

In reality, Marsh exaggerated his claims of danger and high adventure in the West. One of his assistants later wrote that Marsh's "reference to the personal dangers encountered by hostile Indians is amusing in the extreme."[3] Nonetheless, Marsh declared war against Cope. He went to great lengths to make sure that he discovered and named more dinosaurs than Cope did. Marsh recruited a member of Cope's team to act as a spy. The spy told him where Cope was digging and when he was close to a discovery, so that Marsh might be able to beat him to the punch. Marsh also bribed a telegraph operator to tell him of any news that Cope sent back East.

After a few expeditions, Marsh realized that he could collect more fossils by buying them from collectors or by hiring others to do the work than digging them himself. For the most part, he stayed back East, studied the samples that were sent to him, and published his findings.

The dinosaur bone wars heated up to a fever pitch in 1877, thanks to three important finds and an innocent mistake. In April, Arthur Lakes, a schoolteacher from Golden, Colorado, went off on a hike in the mountains near the town of Morrison, Colorado. He came across some huge fossil bones embedded in sandstone. He pried loose the bones of what appeared to be at least six different animals, if not different species. Having heard that Marsh paid well for fossils, Lakes sent ten boxes to Marsh.

When Marsh did not reply, Lakes assumed he was not interested. He sent a few bones to the other well-known purchaser of fossils, Cope. In the meantime, Marsh finally responded. He recognized the bones as belonging to an enormous dinosaur. Enclosed in his letter was a $100 payment for the bones, and a request that Lakes keep his findings a secret until Marsh could publish a paper on the subject.

By that time, Cope was excitedly preparing to publish an article on the bones that Lakes had sent him. Unaware of the feud between Marsh and Cope, Lakes told Cope to send the bones on to Marsh. So it was that Marsh was able to reveal to the world the existence of a huge four-legged dinosaur, which he named *Apatosaurus* (deceptive lizard).

Cope was furious at having these prize bones snatched away and given to his hated rival, but months later, it was his turn to gloat. A collector sent Cope a major fossil discovery unearthed near Canyon City, Colorado. Marsh fumed while Cope took credit for the largest land animal ever found to that point.

While Marsh sent assistants to prowl around the outskirts of Cope's new find, he received a letter from two railroad men (W. E. Carlin and W. H. Reed). While hunting antelope on a high ridge at Como Bluff in southern Wyoming, these men saw large bone fragments sticking out of the ground. They claimed that "the bones extend for seven miles and are by the ton."[4] Marsh rushed money to them to recruit them to his side.

One of the railroad men, William Reed, became one of Marsh's best collectors. The fossil grounds he discovered at Como Bluff yielded more than thirty tons of fossil bones in the first summer. Marsh's crew continued to dig out of Como Bluff an average of a ton of bones per week, for over a decade. All of these bones were sent back to Yale, where Marsh studied them. He decided which bones went together and what the various animals must have looked like. He especially enjoyed naming those that looked different from previously discovered species.

Marsh's diggers discovered twenty-six new species of dinosaurs at Como Bluff. Among their findings was a strange animal with large bony plates on its back. Marsh introduced this creature to the world, giving it the name *Stegosaurus* (covered lizard).

Marsh made a mistake in analyzing one set of bones that causes confusion to this day. He thought he had discovered a new species of huge, four-legged plant eaters. Imagining how the earth must have shaken when this beast lumbered across the land, Marsh named it *Brontosaurus* (thunder lizard). Many years later, scientists discovered that Marsh's *Brontosaurus* was actually the same species as the beast that he earlier had named *Apatosaurus*. The catchy name *Brontosaurus* has caught on among the public, while

This is the skeleton that Marsh named *Brontosaurus*. The specimen stands today in the Great Hall of Yale University's Peabody Museum of Natural History. This photo (taken in 1965) shows the specimen with the incorrect skull, which was later replaced in 1981.

many scientists today insist that *Apatosaurus* is the correct name, since it came first.

In the late 1870s, Marsh also described a fierce meat eater called an *Allosaurus,* and a beast with a tremendously long neck and tail that he called *Diplodocus.* Furthermore, his team unearthed the tiny jaw of a mammal from the same rocks that yielded early dinosaur bones. This proved that mammals had lived on the earth at the same time as the dinosaurs. In the early 1880s, Marsh astounded the world by announcing the discovery in Kansas of giant flying reptiles called pterodactyls whose wingspans measured more than 20 feet (6 meters)!

Piecing together skeletons of animals from a few broken and scattered pieces was a difficult task. One of Marsh's greatest discoveries started off as another piece of mistaken identity. In 1887, U.S. government geologists sent Marsh a pair of giant horn cores that they had found on an expedition. Marsh examined the cores and declared that they belonged to species of extinct bison.

Later that same year, Marsh's assistant, John Bell Hatcher, heard from cattlemen in eastern Wyoming about skulls "with horns as long as a hoe handle and eye holes as big as your hat."[5] Hatcher investigated and found a skull weighing nearly 7 tons (6 metric tons). When Marsh saw the horn core from this beast, he immediately realized that it was from the same animal as his "bison." Marsh named the new horned dinosaur *Triceratops* (three-horned face).

Digging fossils for Marsh was back-breaking work. William Reed once single-handedly dragged a 400-pound (160-kilogram) leg bone more than a mile out of the rocky hills. Another time, he nearly drowned trying to transport bones down an icy creek.

Marsh did little to make the task easier for his assistants and collectors. He often ignored the needs of his assistants and was notoriously tardy in paying their wages. Marsh refused to let his assistants share the credit for his discoveries, and he gave the impression to the world that he had done the fieldwork.

Somehow, Marsh inspired enough loyalty that some of his assistants became as obsessed with the bone wars as Marsh himself. William Reed smashed remaining fossils in a quarry after picking out the best ones, to make sure that Cope would find nothing. On another occasion, Reed sent a landslide of dirt onto the heads of strangers who wandered too close to one of Marsh's quarries.

In many ways, Marsh came out the victor in the bone wars. He described nineteen new types of dinosaurs; Cope described nine. While Cope's fame faded badly in his later years, Marsh enjoyed enormous prestige. He was world famous for his discoveries and held the honored post of president of the National Academy of Sciences for twelve years.

Some historians believe that the fierce rivalry between Marsh and Cope inspired both to achieve far more than they otherwise would have done. While competition spurred Marsh on, however, it eventually ruined his reputation. While Cope was floundering in a sea of financial troubles, Marsh decided to kick his foe while he was down. He used his influence to get the U. S. Department of the Interior to demand that Cope give up his personal fossil collection to the National Museum, where Marsh would have access to it.

That was the last straw for Cope. He struck back by feeding information to a reporter for the *New-York Herald.* The reporter wrote a damaging article about how Marsh took information from his assistants in the field and used it in research papers without ever giving credit. Marsh fired back with a letter to the paper, but it only made him seem mean and petty. The scientific world was outraged over the scandal caused by Marsh and Cope's quarrel.

Marsh further lost support when a member of congress who was up for re-election used him as a scapegoat for government waste, even though Marsh financed almost all of his expeditions with his own money. In 1892, Marsh was forced to resign his prestigious position as fossil expert for the U. S. Geological Survey.

O. C. Marsh did succeed in fulfilling his burning ambition to be the ranking world expert on dinosaurs. He was the man who brought to life the images of some of the world's most beloved dinosaurs— *Apatosaurus, Stegosaurus,* and *Triceratops*—but he paid a steep personal price. He died of pneumonia in 1899, still under the shadow of disgrace for his part in the bitterly contested bone wars.

Edward Drinker Cope

Edward Cope

The Bone Wars, Part II

It takes two to tango, and Edward Cope was every bit as obsessed with beating Marsh to the bones as Marsh was with beating Cope. Cope's personality was at least as difficult as Marsh's. As Cope admitted to his father, "I am not constituted for getting along comfortably with the general run of people."[1] Far more intellectually gifted than Marsh, Cope was impatient with those who did not catch on to things as quickly as he did. He made no effort to spare anyone's feelings, and unleashed a fierce temper whenever he was crossed.

Cope was well on his way to world fame before the famous rivalry started, but the bitter nature of the feud goaded him into a massive effort to outdo

Marsh in discovering dinosaurs. That effort brought Cope both tremendous success and crushing failure.

Edward Drinker Cope was born in 1840 in Fairfield, Pennsylvania, outside of Philadelphia. Like his hated rival, Cope lost his mother at the age of three. Like Marsh, Cope had access to money. His father was a successful shipowner and merchant. A devout Quaker, he gave up his business to devote his life to charity. He sent his children to good Quaker schools.

Unlike Marsh, young Cope was recognized as a scientific marvel. At the age of six, he visited the Philadelphia Academy of Science and made detailed observations of the skeleton of a seafaring dolphin-like reptile called *Ichthyosaurus* (fish lizard). Cope's notes included advanced anatomical terminology, such as his comments on the "bony sclerotic plates in the eye socket."[2]

Although impressed by the boy's understanding of fossils and skeletons, Cope's father saw no practical use for it. He viewed farming as an honest occupation, so he sent Edward to work on a farm during the summers of his teen years. Unfortunately, Edward was more interested in capturing and examining snakes and frogs than in producing farm products.

Cope persuaded his father that Joseph Leidy's lectures on anatomy would help him deal with farm animals. His two years under Leidy were Cope's only formal training in the science of fossils. Through Leidy's influence, Cope joined the Academy of Natural Sciences in Philadelphia. He had his first scientific paper published at the age of eighteen. (Marsh was thirty before he first published.)

Like Marsh, Cope was of prime fighting age during the Civil War. He also sat out the war in Europe. In 1863, his father, who held strong Quaker beliefs opposing war, sent Edward to Europe to study.

Cope returned to the United States late in 1864. He appeared ready to settle down into the solid career that his father laid out for him. He took control of a farm that his father bought for him, and married his distant cousin, Annie Pim. To supplement his income, he accepted a post as professor of zoology at Haverford College, a Quaker school.

Cope quickly made a name for himself with his expert analysis of fossil bones. In 1866, he found a few small fragments of teeth, jaw, and neck bones on the New Jersey coast. From these scraps of evidence, Cope described a small carnivore that he called *Laelaps*, named after a dog in Greek mythology that turned to stone in midleap.

Confident in his ability to support himself by his writing, Cope abandoned his secure career. In 1867, he left the farm, resigned his position as professor, and moved with his wife and daughter to Haddonfield, New Jersey. There he devoted himself to research and writing. He cranked out an impressive number of scientific papers—fifty-six in 1872 alone!

In 1871, Cope traveled for the first time to the

fossil fields of the West. He joined Charles Sternberg in western Kansas on a successful hunt for fossil turtles and sharks.

When Cope's father died in 1875, he left a fortune to his son. This gave Cope the money to compete with O. C. Marsh, with whom he had already begun his bitter feud.

Cope spent more time digging in the ground than either Leidy and Marsh. Despite his rather sheltered upbringing, he showed great stamina. Day after day, Cope trudged over the steep ravines and rocky hills, far from the nearest farm or settlement, from sunup to sundown. The gnats were so fierce that he had to cover his face with bacon grease to repel them. Cope refused to cut short an expedition, even when his scouts and cook abandoned him. Once he stayed out in the fossils fields through the cold, late autumn months, even though he had no warm clothing with him.

On one occasion, Cope stayed out in the field until he was delirious with fever and thirst. He staggered into a fort and, despite his condition, went right to work on a paper describing what he had learned on his expedition.

Cope was either fearless when it came to Native Americans or coolly confident in his ability to judge situations. He found the perfect way to defuse tensions when he happened upon unfriendly Native Americans. Cope would fascinate them by popping out his false teeth and then snapping them back into his mouth.

In the summer of 1876, Cope and Sternberg traveled by train and stagecoach to the barren Montana Badlands. When they arrived, they heard the news that a huge gathering of Plains Indians had just wiped out General George Custer's seventh Cavalry to the last man near the area where Cope intended to look for fossils. The local officials warned Cope that he would commit suicide if he kept to his plans.

Instead of being scared away, Cope proceeded eagerly. It was the perfect time to go into the area, he said. If all the Sioux and their allies were gathered together in one camp, that reduced the chances of his running into small, hostile groups on the rest of the Badlands. Cope took his expedition to within a day's journey of the huge Native American encampment, so close that his local guides deserted him. His judgment was correct—the expedition ran into no problems.

During that summer, Cope and Sternberg unveiled a new type of dinosaur to the world. After studying the unusual head bones, Cope decided that this dinosaur had a horn on its head, much as some modern mammals do. He called the beast *Monoclonius*, a name that refers to its single horn.

A year later came the blockbuster discoveries. In the spring, Lakes uncovered the fossil bed that contained huge bones of *Apatosaurus*. When Lakes sent some samples to Cope, then changed his mind and instructed him to give the bones to Marsh, Cope was furious. One of the great fossil discoveries of all time had been snatched from him.

Cope refused to sit back meekly while Marsh's team pulled its discoveries from Lakes's site. He hired spies to watch the digging and sent workers to hunt for fossils around the edges of Lakes's dig. Cope even bribed some Marsh employees to switch sides and work for him. Nonetheless, Marsh was collecting all the good fossils.

Fortunately for Cope, luck turned his way early in the summer. O.W. Lucas, superintendent of schools at Canyon City, Colorado, went for a hike near Morrison, Colorado. Along the way, he found some unbelievably large fossil bones. As luck would have it, Lucas approached Cope instead of Marsh. When Cope received a sample of bones, he saw at once his chance to turn the tables on Marsh. He encouraged Lucas to keep digging and made arrangements for Lucas to hire a crew. That summer, Lucas and his assistants uncovered the bones of an animal even larger than the *Apatosaurus* that Marsh had so proudly uncovered a few months earlier. Cope originally estimated the beast as being 70 to 88 feet (20 to 25 meters). He later reduced the figure to slightly under 66 feet (20 meters). Even at that, the thick-bodied creature was larger than Marsh's *Apatosaurus*.

Now it was Marsh's turn to counterattack. He sent two of his top assistants to the Canyon City

As nasty as the bone wars got, they goaded Cope and Marsh into collecting a huge mass of bones, and training a generation of scientists to study them.

area to set up new bone quarries. He offered Lucas money to switch sides and fed him stories about how untrustworthy Cope was. Lucas, however, stayed with Cope.

That was the high point of Cope's bone war with Marsh. There were a few other triumphs along the way, though. In the 1880s, David Baldwin found some small, delicate bones in a very ancient stone in New Mexico. Cope analyzed the bones and determined that they were from a small, lightweight meat eater that Cope called *Coelophysis*. This discovery alerted people that dinosaurs came in a wide variety of sizes from little larger than a house cat to a 60-ton (5-metric-ton) mass of flesh. It also gave scientists a clue that dinosaurs lived for an incredibly long time on the earth.

The bone wars ended in disaster for Cope. While he was a genius at piecing together and analyzing fossil bones, he was hopeless at managing money. Even though his father had left him enough money to live on comfortably all his life, Cope fell for a foolish scheme to make even more money. He invested almost all of his fortune in silver mines that turned out to be worthless. With no more money to hire crews and buy fossils, Cope had to drop out of fossil collecting.

Thanks to his wealth and influential connections, Marsh took center stage in the world of fossils and dinosaurs. Cope, meanwhile, tumbled into poverty. He went back to work as a professor at the University of Pennsylvania. In order to pay off his debts, he sold his mammal fossil collection to the American Museum of Natural History in New York. Cope spent his final days on a plain cot in his crowded study in Philadelphia. He died of kidney failure in 1897 at the age of fifty-seven.

While Marsh appeared to come out ahead in the bone wars, Cope far surpassed Marsh in scientific production. During his career, he published more than fourteen hundred scientific articles, including more than six hundred papers on animals with backbones. During his relatively short life, he discovered enough new species to fill an entire museum, nearly thirteen hundred in all. This was more than twice the number of species Marsh described.

More important, however, than the numbers that Cope and Marsh racked up in their selfish competition was the combined effect of the two on the world. Before Marsh and Cope started their work, only nine species of dinosaurs were known to have lived in North America. Together, Marsh and Cope named more than one hundred thirty new species.

While the mean-spirited duel between Marsh and Cope was a blot on the name of science, it had many positive effects. It brought to light a prehistoric world filled with enough strange and exotic creatures to delight and astound everyone from young children to serious scientists.

Henry Fairfield Osborn

Henry Osborn &
Barnum Brown

Tyrannosaurus

Shortly after the Civil War, the showman P. T. Barnum wanted to take advantage of the public's fascination with the newly discovered monsters of the past. He tried to find whole dinosaur skeletons for his American Museum, but the experts told him there were no dinosaur models available. Dinosaur bones were scarce, and the skeletons that had been found were far from complete.

The man who fulfilled Barnum's dream of giving the public a close-up view of prehistoric creatures was Henry Fairfield Osborn. Osborn was born in 1857 in Fairfield, Connecticut, to a wealthy family.

His father was one of the organizers of the Illinois Central Railroad.

Osborn joined the search for dinosaurs more or less out of boredom. While at Princeton University in June 1876, he and two friends took a study break under the shade of a tree. One of them casually commented that they should do something more exciting next summer. Perhaps they could go out west to hunt for dinosaur fossils. To his surprise, the others agreed that it sounded like fun. The next summer, they joined a fossil-hunting expedition to the West. Osborn liked it well enough to sign on for the following two summers as well.

He became so fascinated by the study of ancient life that he sailed to Europe to continue his studies. There he met and studied under some of Europe's finest scientists, including Charles Darwin and Thomas Huxley. When he returned home, he worked with some of the top Americans in his field. This included Edward Cope, whom Osborn called "the most brilliant creative mind in comparative anatomy . . . that America had produced."[1]

Osborn worked as a professor at Columbia University in New York, and took over as president of New York's American Museum of Natural History in 1891. Osborn was a very formal, distinguished man who had an inflated view of himself. On one occasion, he ordered his chauffeur to drive the wrong way down a one-way street in New York City. When a policeman stopped them,

Osborn told him who he was, expecting that his violation would be excused because he was such an important man. On another occasion, he smudged his signature on a document. When an assistant tried to blot it up, Osborn scolded him for tampering with the signature of a great man.

Nonetheless, Osborn was a fine communicator and had a good understanding of the public. His dream was to build the American Museum into a world-class attraction. He was lucky enough to have the support of friends, including one of the richest men in the world, J. P. Morgan. Osborn realized, though, that to fulfill his dream, he needed both scientific backing and public support. Somehow he had to spark interest in his museum.

Dinosaurs, Osborn decided, were just the thing. Although his museum owned no dinosaur bones, Osborn decided he would create the greatest dinosaur exhibit in the world. His first move was to send collectors to western sites including the famous Como Bluff digs. His instructions were to find a big dinosaur skeleton that he could set up at the museum to attract visitors.

Among the collectors that Osborn recruited was Barnum Brown, who, coincidentally, was named after P. T. Barnum. Brown was born in 1873, near Carbondale, Kansas, where his family had recently moved from Wisconsin. Brown's father earned a good living farming and digging and selling the coal on their property.

Osborn and Brown at the dig in Como Bluff

Barnum, the youngest of the Brown children, enjoyed helping his mother in the kitchen. His cooking skills were later useful. In 1889, his father took the sixteen-year-old Barnum with him as cook on a long wagon trip to Montana. The group covered three thousand miles (four thousand eight hundred kilometers) in four months. Brown got a good preview of the empty, dry, rugged land where he would later spend much of his life.

Barnum developed an interest in fossils as a youngster when he found fossils unearthed by the family plow. After attending high school in Lawrence, Kansas (his hometown did not have a high school), he enrolled at the University of Kansas. While he was there, he went on a number of university field trips to collect fossils.

Brown went on to Columbia University for graduate study, but he was always more interested in finding fossils than in studying them in a classroom. Brown was also very good at locating ancient bones. In 1895, he found the well-preserved skull of a *Triceratops.* He returned west to hunt for more fossils the following summer. While out in the field, he ran into an expedition from Osborn's American Museum of Natural History. Brown so impressed them that they asked him to join their party. Brown enjoyed digging for the museum so much that he never did complete his work at Columbia.

During the summer of 1897, Brown and the American Museum of Natural History crew searched the land around the Como Bluff site for fossils. At first, they found so few fossils that they began to suspect this famous dinosaur fossil field had been exhausted by other hunters. Then, on June 14, Brown wrote to Osborn that they had discovered "a veritable gold mine and I have been in bones up to my eyes."[2]

In June of the following year, Brown met with even more spectacular success. Fanning out north of the previous site, he discovered a hillside littered with fossil bones. They were so plentiful that local sheepherders had built a cabin out of bones!

This spot became known as Bone Cabin Quarry. Brown and his team dug out enough bones that summer to fill the two railroad cars donated by J. P. Morgan. The site yielded great numbers of bones of some of the largest dinosaurs, including *Apatosaurus*, *Camarasaurus*, and *Diplodocus*.

In contrast to Marsh and Cope, Brown was cooperative and easy to work with. While Brown was working for the American Museum at the turn of the century, Osborn decided to send him to a promising site overseas in Patagonia, in South America. Despite getting less than a day's notice, Brown accepted the assignment without complaint.

Brown was either incredibly lucky or else had a better sense than other hunters did of where fossils might be. Osborn said of his favorite collector, "Brown is the most amazing collector I have known. He must be able to smell fossils."[3]

Brown's greatest success was due more to hard work and stubborn determination than anything else. In 1902, he took a train to Miles City, in southeastern Montana, still searching for a block-buster find for the American Museum. Brown hired a wagon and team of horses to take him north into the hot, dust-dry Badlands of Montana. After travel-ing five days by wagon, he headed out into land too rugged for a wagon to pass. Surveying an area south of the Missouri River, he observed "this country promises well and has never been examined."[4]

Brown combed through the steep hills and ravines. Eventually, he located fossil bones in a sandstone bluff. The bones appeared to be from a large dinosaur quite different from the four-legged plant eaters such as *Apatosaurus.*

Finding that he had come across a nearly complete skeleton, Brown worked carefully to get the bones out of the hard yellow sandstone without damaging them. Brown used a relatively new invention, dynamite, to blow away the outside rock. As he got closer to the bones, he switched to a pickaxe and then a chisel. The bones were so big, the rock so hard, and the work so delicate that Brown spent the rest of that summer and most of the next trying to pry the bones loose.

Moving the bones from the remote, roadless wilderness back to New York was a backbreaking task. The pelvis weighed about two tons (less than two metric tons) and was too heavy for his wagon.

Brown had to build a sledge and hitch up a team of four strong horses to drag it out of the Hell Creek Valley. It took the horses an entire day to pull the sledge to the nearest road. Once they reached the road, they had 124 more miles (1200 kilometers) of hauling until they reached the nearest railroad.

Brown celebrated the completion of his task by getting married in 1904. A few months later, in 1905, Henry Osborn astounded the world with his report of Brown's find. The bones were those of an enormous 50-foot-long (16-meter) killing machine with a large skull and terrifyingly long sharp teeth. Osborn unveiled a beast so powerful and ferocious that it could devour a human in a bite or two. He named the beast *Tyrannosaurus rex* (king of the tyrant lizards).

In 1908, Brown found another skeleton that gave an even clearer picture of the *Tyrannosaurus.* The skull was nearly 3 feet (90 centimeters) long, with sharp, 6-inch (15-centimeter) teeth. It was so perfectly preserved that Brown remarked that he had never seen anything like it before.

The following year was a tragic one for Brown. Scarlet fever killed his wife, Marion, and attacked his baby daughter. Brown dealt with his grief by leaving the child with his in-laws and heading for the desolate Red Deer River banks of Alberta, Canada. There he dug out an enormous number of fossils. Brown built a barge and floated his huge collection down the river to civilization.

Together, Brown and Osborn succeeded in creating a museum filled with prehistoric wonders that thrilled the public. When they began working for the American Museum of Natural History, the museum had not a single dinosaur skeleton. By the time Osborn retired in 1932, three years before his death, it owned one of the largest and most popular collections in the world. The museum became the showplace of one of the most frightening creatures that ever lived, *Tyrannosaurus rex.*

Barnum Brown lived to be eighty-nine years old. When he died in 1963, he held the reputation of having dug up more dinosaur bones than any other man who ever lived.

Charles H. Sternberg

Charles Sternberg

Family Affair

In the 1860s, Charles H. Sternberg decided that "whatever it might cost me in privation [extreme discomfort], danger, and solitude, I would make it my business to collect facts from the crust of the earth."[1] Little did he know that he was starting a family business.

For the next century, Sternbergs would range throughout western North America in search of dinosaur bones. Despite an injured leg that made walking difficult, Charles roamed the fossil fields for more than sixty years. At times he worked side by side with his three sons, all of whom spent their lives in pursuit of "facts from the crust of the earth."

The long years of hard work were well rewarded. At the age of fifty-eight, Charles came across a discovery beyond anything he had ever hoped for. Instead of the usual bones that revealed the structure of the insides of these great beasts, Sternberg discovered the first solid clue as to what the outside of a dinosaur looked like.

Charles Hazelius Sternberg was born in Otsego County, in upstate New York, in 1850. Charles was raised in a religious atmosphere; his father was principal of a Lutheran seminary. His parents taught him respect and reverence for the natural world.

As a child, Charles suffered a bad fall from a barn loft. This left him with a limp throughout his life, but Charles never let it interfere with his activities. He roamed the outdoors with his twin brother, Edward, and their cousin. They often discovered fossil shells near the house. Charles took careful note of these oddities of nature.

At the age of seventeen, Charles and Edward moved to Ellsworth, Kansas, to help out on the ranch that their older brother owned. While walking on the plains, Charles and Edward came across fossils of leaves. Charles was so delighted by the delicate shapes that he sent the fossils to the United States National Museum in Washington, D. C. He began to build his own fossil collection.

Charles's father tried to discourage him from taking fossil hunting too seriously. He told his son that only rich people could afford to make a career of digging up dinosaur bones, but Charles made up his mind to try. In 1871, he took part in one of

Cope's fossil hunts in Kansas. The following year, he joined a plant fossil expedition. He also enrolled at what is now Kansas State University to get the training he needed.

Charles tried to get hired as one of Marsh's bone finders, but was turned down. It seemed his father was right. With no money of his own and no job offers in sight, Charles turned in desperation to Cope in 1876. He wrote to Cope, promising his undying dedication to fossil hunting. He pleaded for funds to start his own expedition. Cope, who knew nothing about Sternberg beyond this letter, was impressed. He promptly sent Sternberg $300 to get him started.

It was the turning point of Sternberg's life. Cope joined Sternberg that summer, and together they found many interesting fossils. Some of these were so brittle that the men were afraid the bones would fall apart when they sent them back East. Sternberg and Cope solved the problem by leaving some of the bones partially in the rock. They boiled some of the rice they had brought for food into a thick paste. They wrapped strips of paper dipped in this paste around the fossils. This formed a protective cast. The technique worked so well that by 1880, plaster-wrapping of fossils was standard. Virtually all collectors of large vertebrate fossils use a similar method even today.

Although he gave Cope first consideration, Sternberg preferred to work for himself. He became the leading freelance collector of his day. He ranged across the barren lands of the western United States, finding fossils and selling them to North America and European museums.

The work was exhausting and dangerous. Collectors could not carry many supplies through the often impassable lands they search, so Sternberg had to travel light and live off the land. Finding water in those dry lands was the most serious problem, and lack of water almost killed him many times. He battled malaria and other illnesses while spending months prying bones out of rock and preparing them for shipment. When the task of digging was over, he had to solve the problem of getting the fossils back to civilization.

Although he frequently wandered into hostile Native American territory, Sternberg never carried a rifle. "I could not hunt Indians and fossils at the same time," he explained.[2] In fact, he was not the fighting type. In a refreshing contrast to the Marsh-Cope wars, Sternberg made a point of being friendly and polite to rival collectors he met in the field. He figured that there were enough bones for all of them.

Eventually Charles was joined by three sons: George, born in 1883, was his father's chief assistant for many years. Charles M., born in 1885, and Levi, born in 1894, followed. Occasionally, the sons would also go off on their own expeditions, and they even worked for rival collectors such as Barnum Brown.

The sons displayed the same work ethic as their father did. Once, when some fossils were lodged in a tight spot in a ravine, Levi "lay on his back and

Charles H. Sternberg (right) and Lawrence Lambe collected fossils along the Red Deer River in 1912.

patted the plaster-soaked burlap with the ends of his fingers til the blood came out."[3]

Although clashes with Native Americans were no longer a factor when the boys joined Sternberg, they all faced their share of dangers. On one occasion, a huge fossil slid out of control as the Sternbergs tried to lower it downhill into a wagon. Two of the Sternbergs leaped out of the wagon just before the heavy bones demolished it.

There were so many Sternbergs making major fossil finds that people often confused them with each other. One film documentary on the life of Charles M. mistakenly featured George at work in the field.

In 1908, the Sternbergs scoured an unfenced livestock grazing range in southern Wyoming. After a long search, they found an excellent deposit of dinosaur bones. When their party ran out of supplies, Charles Sr. and Charles Jr. went to town and left George and Levi behind. The two remaining Sternbergs decided to work on extracting a few bones lodged in an enormous mass of sandstone.

George and Levi were nearly starving by the time the others returned, but they had found something well worth the effort. "Imagine the feeling that crept over me when I realized that here for the first time, a skeleton of a dinosaur had been discovered wrapped in its skin," said George.[4]

Normally, bacteria eat away all parts of the dinosaur body except the bones. But here was an

Edmontosaurus whose scaly skin had been trapped in the stone and preserved. Charles H. Sternberg was overjoyed when he found what the popular press called the "dinosaur mummy." He called this discovery "the crowning specimen of my life work."[5]

Sternberg, however, experienced crushing defeat as well. During World War I, in the 1920s, money for fossil hunters dried up. Sternberg traveled to Alberta, Canada, to find good specimens for a British museum that had some leftover funds budgeted for fossil collecting. Deep in a narrow gorge, he located two specimens of *Corythosaurus*, a kind of duckbill dinosaur with a bony ridge on its skull. The gorge was too narrow for a horse to enter. Sternberg and his crew cut steps into the rock so that they could drag the 30-foot (9 meter) fossils more than 200 yards (180 meters) to a wagon.

After much effort, Sternberg got his two fine duckbills to the Atlantic Coast. In November 1916, they were loaded onto the *S.S. Mount Temple*. War between the British and Germans was in full swing. On the trip across the Atlantic, German submarines sank the *Mount Temple*. Sternberg's two fossils were lost forever on the ocean bottom.

The loss of the duckbills that he had worked so hard to collect devastated Sternberg, but he continued to seek fossils into his eighties. He died in 1943 at the age of ninety-three. His career and those of his sons were a handsome payoff on Edward Cope's original $300 investment.

Earl Douglass

Earl Douglass
The Public Fossil Field

Earl Douglass was a man with an unusual dream. He thought that people could not get the full idea of what fossil hunting was all about from visiting a museum. Too much happened between the digging and dusting in the field and the sterile, clean exhibits that the public could view. Douglass wanted people to be able to see exactly where the dinosaur bones came from and how they were dug out of the ground. Instead of bringing the fossils to the public, why not bring the public to the fossils?

Earl Douglass was born in Minnesota in 1862. Like O. C. Marsh, Douglass took a long time to complete his education. After starting at the

University of South Dakota, he finally obtained his degree from South Dakota Agricultural College in 1893. He then went on to teach school in Montana.

Like many dinosaur hunters, Douglass grew interested in fossils when he happened upon them while hiking in the outdoors. He was so fascinated by the idea of uncovering ancient remains that he joined a fossil-collecting expedition to Mexico. He then bounced around the country for a few years, trying to find a place for himself in the field of paleontology.

Eventually, in 1902, he landed a job at the Carnegie Museum in Pittsburgh, Pennsylvania. Based by the fortune of the fabulously rich Andrew Carnegie, the museum had just begun to seek its own dinosaur collection. Like Henry Osborn at the American Museum, Carnegie was looking for something spectacular to win the world's attention. He hoped his collectors would bring back a skeleton "as a big as a barn."[1]

Douglass spent his first summers with the Carnegie Museum searching the rugged wilderness of Montana and Utah for fossils. During the winters, he researched and wrote scientific papers about early mammals. Although his papers won praise and respect, nothing spectacular came his way until 1908. That year, Douglass and Carnegie Museum director William Holland loaded up a pair of mules and headed out into the Uinta Range mountains of Utah.

When the footing became difficult, they tied up their mules and went into the gullies and ravines on foot. In order to cover more ground, the two split up. Douglass went right, Holland left. If either found anything interesting, he would summon the other by firing his shotgun.

Before long, Holland heard a shotgun blast. Douglass had found a large *Diplodocus* bone lying out in the open at the bottom of a ravine.

The bone was too large to carry out, and there was no time that summer to start a major dig, but Douglass returned to the site the following year. Unfortunately, the bone appeared to be a fluke. Douglass searched the desolate area from spring until late summer, without finding anything else important.

Then, on August 8, he made the discovery that changed his life. Dinosaur bones often fall apart as the connecting tissue rots. They fall into a heap or are discovered scattered. Douglass found eight *connected* tailbones of a *Apatosaurus*.

Douglass realized that he had come across a treasure chest of dinosaur bones. He saw no point in returning to Pittsburgh for the winter to write and do research when there was so much to do at this newly discovered Carnegie Quarry. Douglass decided to live on the site and devote his life to developing it. He stopped writing scientific papers. Instead he spent his time trying to get roads constructed, buying tools, and lining up a crew to work the following summer.

Earl Douglass stands in front of a rich find of dinosaur bones. This find would later become part of Dinosaur National Monument which stretches across Colorado and Utah.

Douglass also wrote home with a bold request. He asked his wife, Pearl, to bring their one-year-old son out with her so they could make their home at the site. The prospect could not have been appealing. A bleak, dry, wind-swept quarry twenty miles (thirty-two kilometers) from the nearest town was not the most inviting place to raise an infant, but Pearl accepted the challenge.

The family toughed out the first winter. They slept in a tent and spent the days in a wood frame covered with canvas. An iron stove was their only protection against the -30°F (-35°C) winter chill.

Rather than being discouraged by the harsh conditions, the family settled there permanently. Earl built a solid log house. He tried to set up a small farm with cows and chickens so that the family could produce all the food it needed. In an effort to get the water he needed for the farm, he built a dam across a gulley. Douglass's father and sister were intrigued by the back-to-nature situation and came out to join him. The farm never worked out the way Douglass hoped. Even with the dam, the land was too dry to support much more than a small garden, but the Douglass family stayed anyway.

Once Douglass got his quarry going, he and his crew worked throughout the year in all but the worst weather. Douglass supervised the digging during the day. He spent hours at night filling his notebook with observations and illustrations.

Douglass and his crew used dynamite to blast

away layers of rock reach the dinosaur bones. They produced so much rock debris that Douglass got a mining railroad car to haul it away. Between 1909 and 1922, Douglass's crew removed enough sandstone to create a 600-foot-long (190-meter) trench 80 feet (24 meters) deep. In the process, they uncovered over 700,000 pounds (318,000 kilograms) of fossils, by far the richest dinosaur quarry ever found up to that time. Carnegie Quarry yielded the complete or nearly complete skeletons of twenty individual dinosaurs, including a very rare juvenile *Camarasaurus.* Mixed in with those skeletons were the bones of four hundred other dinosaurs, including *Apatosaurus, Stegosaurus,* and *Allosaurus.*

Perhaps the most spectacular find was that of a complete *Diplodocus* skeleton. Stretching out to nearly 100 feet (38 meters), it was exactly the "big as a barn" specimen that Andrew Carnegie had been hoping for.

While collecting all those specimens, Douglass wondered why so many skeletons were buried in one place. He studied the rock formations and the positions of the bones when they were found. He noticed that the bones in the upper layers were widely scattered, while the lower bones had stayed together. Douglass concluded that this was not a death pit that dinosaurs fell into. Instead, it was probably a sandbar in a river. The dinosaurs died near a river and floated downstream until they were caught on the bar. More sand washed downstream and covered up the bones. Those that were covered first by the sand deposits would likely be intact. Those not covered right away were more likely to be washed away by the current and scattered.

A few years after Douglass started work at the quarry, he began to worry about the future of the quarry. The site was on federal land in an area open for settlement. If somebody bought the land, they could end work at the quarry. In an effort to protect the quarry, Douglass tried to get mining rights to the land, but the government ruled that fossils were not covered by mining laws.

Some influential friends took Douglass's concern to President Woodrow Wilson. In 1915, Wilson reserved eighty acres on which the quarry stood as Dinosaur National Monument, under the protection of the government.

Douglass was pleased, but at the same time he imagined an even greater plan for the quarry. Wouldn't it be wonderful if the public could see dinosaur bones right where fossil hunters had found them? Douglass saw that the Carnegie Quarry was perfect for this idea. The layer of sandstone in which most of the bones were located was steeply slanted. This made it easy for people to view a whole layer of dinosaur bones at once.

For eight years, Douglass was too busy to pursue this goal, but in 1933, the Carnegie Museum stopped financing the dig. Douglass stayed behind, refusing to abandon the work that had become his life. He began campaigning for his "exhibition in

Although well off the beaten path, Dinosaur National Monument attracts many thousands of visitors each summer.

place," as he called it. "I hope the Government, for the benefit of science and the people, will uncover a large area, leave the bones, and skeletons in relief and house them in. It would make one of the most astounding and instructive sights imaginable."[2]

Not until 1933 did the government take his proposal seriously. At that time, some work was done to prepare it for visitors, but the work was interrupted as other matters took priority for government officials. Finally, in 1958, a greatly expanded Dinosaur Monument opened to the public. Douglass's dream had come true—part of the quarry lay behind a glass-walled building. There visitors can see the dinosaur bones as they were found and gain a better understanding of how dinosaur hunters work.

Roy Chapman Andrews

Roy Chapman Andrews
The Original Indiana Jones

"A thousand screaming demons seemed to be pelting my face with sand and gravel," wrote the adventurer.[1] The storm that roared out of the Gobi Desert sandblasted his car windshield until he could no longer see through it. In his quest for ancient materials buried in the crust of the earth, the man ran into nests of poisonous snakes, fought gun battles with bandits, and wheedled and bribed his way past corrupt government officials. Easily recognizable in his broad-brimmed hat, he relished adventures that would send the average person racing for the safety of home.

This description seems to fit the fictional movie character named Indiana Jones. In fact, the swashbuckling adventurer described above was a real-life fossil hunter named Roy Chapman Andrews. Although dinosaur hunters accept physical hardship as part of the job, few of them have faced the trials and dangers encountered by Andrews.

Roy Chapman Andrews was born in Beloit, Wisconsin, in 1884. From the time he was a child, he knew he wanted to be a naturalist. His goal in life was to get a job at the American Museum of Natural History.

Andrews attended college in Wisconsin and supported himself by stuffing and mounting animals. In 1906, he headed to New York, determined to join the staff of the American Museum. When he was told there were no openings, he offered to scrub floors for the museum until something came up.

Eventually the museum found a more interesting task for the floor-scrubber. Andrews was asked to make a whale model exhibit. He accepted the job with enthusiasm, collecting whale skeletons from around the world. In the meantime, he continued his studies at Columbia University where he earned his master's degree and doctorate.

Andrews had a gift for communicating. His articles and books were popular and he attracted large audiences for his slide lectures. Looking for more experiences for his storytelling, he and his wife visited the Gobi Desert of Mongolia in 1919. Andrews was looking for unusual mammals, but he found something quite unexpected. "I found my country," Andrews exclaimed. "The one I had been born to know and love."[2] The harsh desert country might have discouraged most visitors, but it appealed to Andrews's spirit of adventure.

In 1920, Andrews approached his boss, Henry Osborn, about organizing an expedition to Mongolia. Osborn agreed that there might be some interesting fossils hidden in the sands of the Gobi. He was intrigued by the possibility of finding a "missing link"—a skull of a prehuman creature that would clearly show how humans evolved from other species.

Andrews proposed a new approach. Rather than sending a small crew of diggers to find and send fossil finds back to the experts, he suggested sending a large team of highly trained specialists to collect animals, fossils, and cultural remains.

Such an expedition was expensive, but within a year, Osborn and Andrews had raised the necessary money. In April 1921, the largest and most publicized fossil expedition of all time left the United States for the wilds of Mongolia. In Mongolia, Andrews formed a caravan of cars, trucks, and 125 camels to carry supplies.

Andrews took an enormous risk. The Mongolians, many of whom had never seen a car before, were suspicious of the expedition. Andrews constantly met with officials trying to get permission to carry out his exploration. Occasionally, he had to pay bribes.

Roving bandits were a serious problem. They murdered one member of the expedition. Andrews

Andrews discovered fossil dinosaur eggs in the Mongolian desert.

drove off several attacks with gunfire. On one occasion, Andrews was off by himself on a scouting mission when three mounted thieves closed in on him. Andrews got in his car and charged the three, scattering them.

The desert posed a different kind of threat. Temperatures soared as high as 140°F (60°C) in the sun and 110°F (43°C) in the shade during the summer. In the winter, the thermometer plunged to -50°F (-45°C) Windstorms churned the desert into a blinding fury.

Even if the expedition survived the dangers, hardships, and equipment breakdowns, they ran the risk of coming home empty-handed. Critics scoffed that Andrews might as well look in the Pacific Ocean for fossils as the empty Gobi Desert. For a while, the critics appeared to be right. Andrews's expedition found little of value during their early searches.

When Andrews heard reports of dinosaur bones in a region, he sent some people to check it out. While one of the investigators was setting up a tent, he had trouble pounding a stake into the hard ground. He thought he had struck a rock, but it turned out to be a dinosaur bone. The man kept running into bones every time he tried to pound the stake into a new section of ground. By the time the tent was pitched, he had discovered more than fifty bones!

Later that summer, Andrews explored an area of

badlands that was just as rich in fossils. According to Andrews, he was finding dinosaurs almost everywhere he looked. Andrews was pleased to find a wonderfully preserved skull of a *Protoceratops*, an ancestor of the *Triceratops*. According to his assistants, Andrews got a little too excited when he discovered fossils. He was so impatient to collect the fossil and get moving to the next one that he was sometimes careless. His fellow workers privately described chipped or damaged fossils as having been "RCA'd," in reference to Andrews's initials.

Andrews never did find the "missing link" that Osborn hoped for but he found other fossils just as spectacular. The expedition's most important find came by accident. During one long day's journey in the desert, the caravan stopped for a break. The group's photographer took a walk to stretch his legs. He stumbled on a dinosaur skull, which was unusual, but what really attracted the expedition's interest was a partially broken eggshell.

Andrews could not believe his luck. Until that time, no one knew for certain how the dinosaurs reproduced. Many suspected that they laid eggs like those of modern reptiles and birds, but no one had ever found any dinosaur eggs. This oblong object, 8 inches (20 centimeters) long and 7 inches (18 centimeters) around, clearly had to be a dinosaur egg.

Andrews and his crew combed the area for more specimens. They found a block of sandstone that contained thirteen eggs in two layers. Andrews also found tiny skulls that turned out to the oldest mammal bones ever found up to that time.

Word of Andrews's discoveries and hair-raising adventures reached the United States before he did. When his ship arrived in Seattle in October 1923, reporters were crowding the dock. They offered him thousands of dollars for the exclusive right to photograph his dinosaur egg. At Andrews's first lecture upon returning home, four thousand people tried to cram into a fourteen-hundred seat auditorium to hear him.

The first expedition's success led Andrews to go back to Mongolia again and again. He continued to find clever ways to raise money and to keep his projects in the public eye. In early 1924, the American Museum announced the sale of a dinosaur egg to raise money for the next trip. A generous backer paid $5,000 for the egg.

Unfortunately, this got Andrews in trouble with the Mongolian and Chinese authorities. When they heard how much a single egg brought in, they decided Andrews was plundering the Gobi of valuable items. They followed his every move when he returned to the desert in 1925.

Eventually, the Gobi expeditions discovered more than one hundred skeletons of *Protoceratops*. These were especially valuable because they showed the animal in all stages of growth, from eggs to babies to juveniles to adult. For the first time, scientists had an accurate view of the life cycle of a dinosaur.

The Andrews expedition also discovered a fierce, swift predator that they named *Velociraptor*. They found so many fossils that they ran out of supplies needed to package them safely. When the burlap strips ran out, the crew tore up their underwear, shirts, and pajamas to use instead.

During the late 1920s, the resistance from Mongolian and Chinese officials increased. The government accused Andrews of being an opium smuggler and a spy. They even seized his fossil collection. Andrews argued and pleaded for six weeks until the fossils were returned to him.

In 1931, the problems finally became too great. Andrews gave up and returned home. Depressed over having to abandon his great expedition, he accomplished little. He took over as head of the American Museum of Natural History when Osborn retired in 1934. When the museum fell on hard times, Andrews took most of the blame. Museum directors forced him to resign in 1941.

Andrews spent the last nineteen years of his life reliving the past. He wrote books about the expeditions including *Across Mongolian Plains, On the Trail of Ancient Man,* and an autobiography, *Under A Lucky Star,* and gave talks about his great adventures in the Gobi Desert and about dinosaurs. As always, Andrews made a scientific expedition sound like an adventure novel, with himself as the rugged hero. After describing a series of disasters and terrible hardships that he faced in Mongolia, Andrews cooly shrugged them off as "all part of a day's work."[3] The most swashbuckling of all dinosaur detectives died in 1960 at the age of seventy-six in Carmel, California.

Robert Bakker

Robert Bakker
Upsetting the Old Theories

For more than a century after the first dinosaur fossil was identified in North America, dinosaur detectives worked primarily on reconstructing skeletons, and naming new species. Their job was to find actual pieces of dinosaurs and to determine how those pieces fit together.

Robert Bakker, however, was fascinated by a detective task more difficult than simply piecing bones together. He wanted to know about the parts of the dinosaur that fossils could not preserve, such as the heart and brain. He wanted to know what dinosaurs were like, how they lived, and why they ruled the world for so long. A full-bearded, ponytailed rebel, Bakker enjoyed challenging some of the most widely accepted "facts" about dinosaurs.

He took special aim at the established view that dinosaurs were cold-blooded animals like lizards. According to Bakker's investigation, dinosaurs were actually warm-blooded, birdlike creatures.

Robert Bakker was born in 1945, in Ridgewood, New Jersey. When he was ten, he paged through an issue of *Life* magazine while visiting his grandfather. An article called "The World We Live In" attracted his attention. The article contained a foldout color illustration of a green *Apatosaurus* plodding through a prehistoric swamp. Bakker was so fascinated by the image of the enormous beast that he instantly decided to devote his life to studying dinosaurs.

After that, Bakker went twice a year with his mother to visit the American Museum of Natural History in New York. No one took the youngster's interest in dinosaurs seriously. According to Bakker, "my family and the doctor predicted it was just a hormonal stage that would pass."[1]

Bakker's interest in dinosaurs only got stronger. He went on to study paleontology at Yale University in the 1960s. Bakker was a member of John Ostrom's crew that discovered a meat-eating dinosaur similar to a *Velociraptor*. Ostrom named the animal *Deinonychus* (terrible claw) because of the large, sharp claw on each of its feet.

Bakker kept studying dinosaurs until he obtained his doctorate. He continued to enjoy digging for bones and had a mysterious knack for knowing where the fossils might be. One quarry crew was growing discouraged at not being able to find any fossils. Bakker showed up and almost immediately found a jawbone, then more fossils. "They thought I belonged to a secret religion." Bakker later chuckled.[2] Bakker also became an expert at comparing the bone structures of various creatures.

Bakker enjoyed sharing his knowledge of dinosaurs. He taught classes to people of all ages, from kindergartners to adults.

While working at Yale's Peabody Museum, Bakker was hit with an inspiration as powerful as the one that had first made him interested in dinosaurs. It was 3:00 A.M., and the room was deserted. While looking at the *Apatosaurus* skeleton in the dead stillness of the museum, Bakker suddenly got a funny feeling. The skeleton was put together exactly as the experts said it should be, yet something was wrong with the picture.

Bakker looked carefully at the bone joints. The limbs on the skeleton were connected as lizards' would be. Lizard limbs sprawl out from the side of the body. They are not packed tight to the body like a horse's legs. Bakker's experience, however, told him that a *Apatosaurus* leg was not like a lizard leg.

Bakker thought of the image of dinosaurs as slow, dumb, plodding overgrown lizards. They were failures, according to the common wisdom. They were so slow and clumsy and unable to adapt that they became extinct.

Bakker suddenly realized what the problem was.

Dinosaurs were actually an incredible success story. They were amazingly successful creatures that had dominated the earth for 165 million years. Bakker saw that the image of dinosaurs as clumsy, outdated lizards was wrong. In fact, based on his understanding of limbs, dinosaurs were very different from lizards.

Bakker realized that he could not understand dinosaurs simply by collecting dinosaur bones. In order to really see what dinosaurs were like, he said, "You have to take them apart as if you never saw one."[3] He dissected frogs, toads, bats, dogs, alligators, and other creatures. He made note of how dinosaurs were similar to those creatures and how they were different.

His discoveries led him to doubt much of the accepted information about dinosaurs. As a twenty-three-year-old, Bakker made his first major impact on the scientific world with a controversial paper. In it, Bakker tried to prove that dinosaurs were not slow, lumbering swamp dwellers as was widely supposed. The *Apatosaurus* did not need water to help support its weight. "If dinosaurs were really slow-moving mountains of cold-blooded flesh, how did they manage to suppress speedy, warm-blood mammals for millions of years?" he asked.[4]

As Bakker began to consider just what dinosaurs were, he noticed more similarities with birds than with reptiles. Actually, this was not a new idea. Sir

Richard Owen, the Englishman who coined the word *dinosaur* in the mid-nineteenth century, commented on the resemblance between birds and early dinosaurs. In the 1860s, another Englishman, Thomas Huxley, argued that birds could be descended from dinosaurs. He went so far as to propose dinosaurs might have been warm-blooded.

That line of thinking had fallen out of favor. In 1975, Bakker published an article in *Scientific American* that brought back the notion that dinosaurs gave rise to birds. In fact, Bakker flatly declared that many dinosaurs were warm-blooded like birds and mammals and not cold-blooded like modern reptiles.

Bakker's article drew a storm of criticism from scientists who held to the old reptile view of dinosaurs. "Taking dinosaurs out of the reptiles is like burning a flag," Bakker noted.[5] Bakker decided that as long as the established scientists were scorning him, he might as well make a complete break with them. Bakker took his case to the public. He wrote a book called *Dinosaur Heresies,* in which he laid out the case for fast, mobile, warm-blooded dinosaurs that lived on dry land, not in swamps.

Many of Bakker's arguments compared the dinosaurs to creatures of today. Which are the largest animals today, cold-blooded or warm-blooded? Obviously, warm-blooded elephants and bison are much larger than the biggest cold-blooded lizard. The fossil record shows that dinosaurs grew fast. Which grow faster today, warm-blooded or cold-blooded animals? Warm-blooded animals do.

Critics responded that warm-blooded animals require more food than cold-blooded animals do. Dinosaur heads, they said, were too small to allow them to eat enough to support a warm-blooded body. Bakker noted that many modern birds with large bodies and small heads can digest a great deal of food, because they depend on gizzard stones to grind their food.

Bakker pointed to worn teeth and long necks in plant eaters as proof that dinosaurs lived on dry land. If they lived in swamps and ate mushy water plants, why would their teeth be worn? What was the purpose of a long neck unless the animal needed it to reach into the trees?

What about speed and quickness? Bakker observed that small dinosaurs were able to compete successfully with similar-sized mammals for millions of years. How could they have done so unless they were at least as fast and nimble as the mammals? Bakker found that the legs of *Triceratops* were built more like those of a powerful, fast mammal than like those of a slow tortoise. It must have been able to run at least as fast. In Bakker's view, even the traditional green swampy color of dinosaurs was wrong. He observed that both birds and crocodiles can see colors. It was logical to suppose that dinosaurs could see colors also. Perhaps many of them were brilliantly colored as a means of attracting others of their species, just as birds are.

Bakker further upset paleontologists by taking shots at their way of communicating. Bakker scoffed at scientists who insisted that the proper name for a *Brontosaurus* was *Apatosaurus.* To him, that was a case of scientists using stuffy jargon instead of trying to communicate effectively. Most people were familiar with the name *Brontosaurus;* therefore, that was the name scientists should use. Bakker's eagerness to speak in language that ordinary people understood paid off. His book became a best-seller.

Many paleontologists remained unconvinced of Bakker's claims. Critics lashed out at him for stating his unproven guesses as if they were fact. Bakker shook his head and said his critics were still living in the Dark Ages. Whether he won supporters or outraged his critics, Bakker stirred up tremendous interest in dinosaurs. Great debates raged over whether Bakker was right or wrong.

Bakker's detective work was largely responsible for constructing a whole new image of those ancient beasts. He turned the lights out on a swampy world of green, dim-witted, sluggish reptiles. He has helped bring into view a far more fascinating world of the colorful, galloping, quick and able creatures who once ruled the earth.

Jack Horner

Jack Horner

The Good Mother Dinosaur

While Robert Bakker was making his impact on the scientific world in the early 1970s, Jack Horner was flunking out of college. Unable to handle his course work, he went back home to Shelby, Montana. There he drove a truck for the family gravel business.

No one would have suspected that within ten years, Horner would be heading the largest fossil research team in the United States. While dyslexia, a reading disability, prevented him from being a top student, Horner was a master detective. He could extract crucial information from the most unlikely sources. All he needed to shake up the scientific world was a lucky break to get started.

Horner grew up in Shelby, a town near the

Alberta border. He became interested in dinosaurs when he found some fossils at the age of seven. Horner began hunting fossils and organizing a collection.

By the time he reached high school, Horner had narrowed his career goals to two possibilities: rocket scientist or paleontologist. He amazed his classmates and teachers by building and launching a rocket that soared 15,000 feet (4,500 meters) at 800 miles (1,300 kilometers) per hour. Because of his dyslexia, he got poor grades and gave up on rocket science.

Horner enjoyed biology and geology classes at the University of Montana and even took graduate courses in those areas, but he did not pass other courses that he needed to get his degree. After seven years of trying, Horner left school, served in Vietnam, and then joined his brother in operating the family sand and gravel business.

Horner continued to pursue his goal of working with dinosaur fossils. He wrote to every natural history museum in the English-speaking world, without success. He joined the Society of Vertebrate Paleontology. Through contacts in this organization, he finally landed a job as a preparator at Princeton University, in 1975. His job was to clean up the fossils found by others and to make them presentable.

Horner was especially interested in the duckbill fossils such as those he had found in Montana as a youth. In the summer of 1977, he went fossil hunting with his dad in western Montana. He found a lump of rock that looked like a crushed dinosaur bone. The object turned out to be one of the first intact dinosaur eggs found in North America.

Although Horner was pleased with the find, he thought little about it. According to Horner, "Until the winter of 1978, I'd had no particular interest in baby dinosaurs."[1] Then Horner became curious when he discovered that most baby dinosaur remains had been found in only one particular type of rock. Outside of Andrews's Mongolian expedition, no one had found any major sources of baby dinosaur bones. Why not?

Some scientists thought that baby dinosaur bones were scarce because they were so small and delicate. They probably disintegrated more easily than adult bones did. If that were the case, Horner pointed out, why were the equally small and delicate bones of smaller ancient reptiles so easily found?

Horner found that most dinosaur fossils found in ocean sediment were duckbills, even though duckbills were land creatures. That meant that duckbills possibly lived near the ocean and were washed into the sea. Horner wondered if the absence of babies in marine deposits meant that the babies lived somewhere else. He noted that a number of modern animals travel outside their usual habitat to lay eggs. Perhaps the duckbills did so. If they went to the upper coastal plains to lay eggs, no wonder baby fossils were so rare. In the steeper upper plains, bones were more likely to be washed or blown away rather than to be covered with soil that would preserve them.

Horner decided to stop searching the rocks of the ancient marine deposits, where paleontologists usually searched. Instead, he searched in more inland deposits. Since he was not paid to hunt for fossils, his only chance to test his theory was during his vacation. During the summer of 1978, he went hunting with his good friend Bob Makela for baby duckbills in the Billings, Montana, area. They found nothing.

While he was on his way to a new site to the northwest, Horner heard of rock shop owners in Bynum, Montana, who had fossils they wanted identified. Horner took a detour to the home of Marian and John Brandvold. They brought out some small bones they had collected the spring before. Horner recognized the hip end of a duckbill thigh bone and a rib bone—only these were tiny versions of those bones! The thigh bone was no bigger than Horner's thumb. The Brandvolds then brought out a coffee can filled with such miniature bones, including a duckbill jaw. The jaw, which normally reached 3 feet (90 centimeters), was only about two inches (less than one centimeter) long.

Horner learned that these bones had come from a ranch near Choteau, Montana. The rocks there were about two hundred miles (three hundred kilometers) inland from the coastline of the ancient sea. Perhaps Horner's theory about dinosaurs migrating to lay eggs was right!

Horner called back to Princeton with news of what he had found. His boss immediately sent him $500 for expenses and told him to check out the location.

That summer, Horner and Makela found a depression in the earth. It was filled with "a bunch of black, sticklike rocks," according to Horner.[2] These rocks turned out to be eggs, and the depression was a fossil nest, 6 feet (2 meters) in diameter. This was the first evidence that dinosaurs built nests to lay their eggs.

Using a garden hose and window screen to separate fossils from ordinary rock, Horner discovered the remains of fifteen baby duckbills in the nest. He knew from the incompletely formed bones that they were babies, but the larger of these youngsters had worn teeth. Furthermore, Horner found finely crushed eggshells in the nest. Near the nest, he found fossils of adult duckbills.

Horner put the pieces of this puzzle together in a way that rocked the scientific world. The finely crushed shells indicated that the babies had trampled the eggs. In order to do that, they had to have spent a great deal of time in the nest. The worn teeth indicated that these youngsters had been eating solid food for some time. Babies could not survive in a nest for several months unless an adult duckbill was feeding them. Horner demonstrated what no one had suspected—that duckbills took care of their young. Horner and Makela named this type of duckbill *Maiasaurus* (good mother lizard).

In this recreation, a maiasaur feeds its young.

Horner assembled a crew of thirteen, mostly volunteers, to help him dig out more fossils from this nesting site. Because the pieces they were looking for were so small, this search was more difficult than many other fossil digs. The searchers had to bend over, with their eyes less than two feet from the ground, in order to spot the fossils. The crew worked six days out of seven in the burning sun, with no luxuries such as bathrooms or running water.

Eventually they discovered valuable clues about the maiasaur's lifestyle. They found a cluster of nests about twenty-five feet (eight meters) apart. From the way these were located in the rock, Horner concluded that all were from the same breeding period. Apparently, maiasaurs had flocked to this location in a large group to lay their eggs. Horner's group then found nests in different layers of rock. This showed that maiasaurs returned to the same breeding ground year after year as migrating birds do.

One year the crew discovered eggs on what had been an island in an ancient shallow lake. These were not the eggs of *Maiasaurus* but of a different type of dinosaur called a hypsilophodontid. "There are spots where, without ever digging, you can literally shovel up the baby bones," said Horner.[3] He estimated that there might have been as many as five hundred nests at that breeding spot.

Horner's discoveries provided solid evidence for Bakker's claim that dinosaurs were birdlike and warm-blooded. "The fact that numerous baby hadrosaurs had been eating and staying together suggests the presence of extended parental care comparable to that practiced by warm-blooded animals," he observed.[4] No modern reptiles share food with their young the way these duckbills did. On the other hand, most birds bring food to their young.

Furthermore, Horner and his crews found bones ranging in size from 14 inches (35 centimeters) to nearly 3 feet (almost a meter). He noted that cold-blooded creatures such as crocodiles require a year to double in size. No cold-blooded creature in nature keeps its young in a nest and provides it with food for an entire year. The only way the dinosaurs could have grown fast enough to double in size and still get out of the nest in a reasonable amount of time was if they were warm-blooded.

In 1984, Horner made one of the most colossal finds in fossil history. His crew uncovered a tomb containing an estimated 30 million fragments of fossils. Horner estimated that the remains of at least ten thousand maiasaurs were buried at that site, not a single baby among them. The question was: What great disaster could have killed so many dinosaurs?

Horner studied the clues. Although the bones were in poor condition, they were not chewed. The largest bones were at the center of the mass of bones, the smallest at the edges. A fine layer of volcanic ash lay over the fossils.

Horner agreed with a graduate student's suggestion

that the herd was killed by gases from an erupting volcano. The heat and smoke were so unbearable that no carnivores or scavengers could get at the bodies before a flood covered the grave and washed the smallest bones a short distance away.

Horner went on to teach at Montana State University and work as the curator of paleontology at the Museum of the Rockies. Many people learned about him because of his famous role as a consultant to the movie *Jurassic Park*. Scientists, though, remember him as the man who uncovered more information about a single species of dinosaur than any paleontologist in history.

Chapter Notes

Introduction

1. William Matthews III, "American Fossil Hunters," *Earth Science*, Spring 1990, p. 16.

Chapter 1

1. David A.E. Spalding, *Dinosaur Hunters* (Rocklin, Calif.: Prima, 1993), p. 60.

2. Ibid., p. 84.

3. Edwin H. Colbert, *The Great Dinosaur Hunters and Their Discoveries* (New York: Dover, 1984), p. 41.

4. Ibid., p. 38.

Chapter 2

1. David A.E. Spalding, *Dinosaur Hunters* (Rocklin, Calif.: Prima, 1993), p. 88.

2. Edwin H. Colbert, *The Great Dinosaur Hunters and Their Discoveries* (New York: Dover, 1984), p. 47.

Chapter 3

1. Edwin H. Colbert, *The Great Dinosaur Hunters and Their Discoveries* (New York: Dover, 1984), p. 101.

2. Ibid.

3. David A.E. Spalding, *Dinosaur Hunters* (Rocklin, Calif.: Prima, 1993), p. 98.

4. Ibid., p. 102.

5. Ibid., p. 120.

Chapter 4

1. Edwin H. Colbert, *The Great Dinosaur Hunters and Their Discoveries* (New York: Dover, 1984), p. 98.

Chapter 5

1. David A.E. Spalding, *Dinosaur Hunters* (Rocklin, Calif.: Prima, 1993), p. 107.

2. Joseph Wallace, *The American Natural History Museum's Book of Dinosaurs and Other Ancient Creatures* (New York: Simon and Schuster, 1994), p. 23.

3. Spalding, p. 126.

4. Ibid.

Chapter 6

1. Edwin H. Colbert, *The Great Dinosaur Hunters and Their Discoveries* (New York: Dover, 1984), p. 110.

2. Ibid., p. 113.

3. David A.E. Spalding, *Dinosaurs Hunters* (Rocklin, Calif.: Prima, 1993), p. 153.

4. Ibid., p. 127.

5. Ibid.

Chapter 7

1. Edwin H. Colbert, *The Great Dinosaur Hunters and Their Discoveries* (New York: Dover, 1984), p. 164.

2. Ibid., p. 169.

Chapter 8

1. David A.E. Spalding, *Dinosaur Hunters* (Rocklin, Calif.: Prima, 1993), p. 211.

2. Ibid., p. 216.

3. Joseph Wallace, *The American Natural History Museum's Book of Dinosaurs & Other Ancient Creatures* (New York: Simon and Schuster, 1994), p. 48.

Chapter 9

1. John N. Wilford, *The Riddle of the Dinosaur* (New York: Vintage, 1987), p. 8.

2. Vicki Lindner, "Interview," *Omni*, March 1992, p. 66.

3. Ibid.

4. Ibid., p. 64.

5. Ibid.

Chapter 10

1. John Horner, *Digging Dinosaurs* (New York: Workman, 1988), p. 23.

2. Richard Conniff, "Head Man in the Boneyard," *Time*, September 10, 1990, p. 78.

3. Horner, p. 172.

4. David A.E. Spalding, *Dinosaur Hunters* (Rocklin, Calif.: Prima, 1993), p. 208.

Further Reading

Bakker, Robert. *Dinosaur Heresies*. New York: William Morrow, 1986.

Colbert, Edwin H. *The Great Dinosaur Hunters and Their Discoveries*. New York: Dover, 1984.

Conniff, Richard. "Head Man in the Boneyard." *Time*, September 10, 1990, p. 78.

Horner, John. *Digging Dinosaurs*. New York: Workman, 1988.

Lindner, Vicki. "Interview." *Omni*, March 1992, p. 66.

Matthews, William, III. "American Fossil Hunters." *Earth Science*, Spring 1990, p. 16.

Spalding, David A.E. *Dinosaur Hunters*. Rocklin, Calif.: Prima, 1993.

Wallace, Joseph. *The American Museum of Natural History Book of Dinosaurs and Other Ancient Creatures*. New York: Simon and Schuster, 1994.

Wilford, John. *The Riddle of the Dinosaur*. New York: Vintage, 1987.

Index